World War 2

Women

Incredible Stories And Accounts Of World War 2 Women Spies, Heroes And Informers

Book 2

© Copyright 2015 by Cyrus J. Zachary - All rights reserved.

This document is geared towards providing exact and reliable information in regards to the topic and issue covered. The publication is sold with the idea that the publisher is not required to render accounting, officially permitted, or otherwise, qualified services. If advice is necessary, legal or professional, a practiced individual in the profession should be ordered.

- From a Declaration of Principles which was accepted and approved equally by a Committee of the American Bar Association and a Committee of Publishers and Associations.

In no way is it legal to reproduce, duplicate, or transmit any part of this document in either electronic means or in printed format. Recording of this publication is strictly prohibited and any storage of this document is not allowed unless with written permission from the publisher. All rights reserved.

The information provided herein is stated to be truthful and consistent, in that any liability, in terms of inattention or otherwise, by any usage or abuse of any policies, processes, or directions contained within is the solitary and utter responsibility of the recipient reader. Under no circumstances will any legal responsibility or blame be held against the publisher for any reparation, damages, or monetary loss due to the information herein, either directly or indirectly.

Respective authors own all copyrights not held by the publisher.

The information herein is offered for informational purposes solely, and is universal as so. The presentation of the information is without contract or any type of guarantee assurance.

The trademarks that are used are without any consent, and the publication of the trademark is without permission or backing by the trademark owner. All trademarks and brands within this book are for clarifying purposes only and are the owned by the owners themselves, not affiliated with this document.

Cover image courtesy of Flickr - https://www.flickr.com/photos/nationalmuseet/6045795926/

Table of Contents

Table of Contents	iv
Introduction	vi
Chapter 1: Pearl Witherington – The Leading Lady	1
Chapter 2: Virginia Hall – The Limping Lady	15
Chapter 3: Krystyna Skarbek – The Woman With Many Faces	22
Chapter 4: Noor Inayat Khan – The Warrior Princess	41
Conclusion	53
Other Books Written By Me	55

Like FREE books?

Would you like them delivered to you every week?

Do you like non-fiction books on a huge range of different topics?

We send out FREE e-books every week so we can share our books with the world!

We have FREE books every week on AMAZON that we send to our email list.

So if you want in, then visit the link at the end of this book to sign up and sit back and wait for new books to be sent straight to your inbox!

World War Two Women

Introduction

I want to thank you for purchasing the book, "World War 2 Women - Incredible Stories And Accounts Of World War 2 Women Spies, Heroes And Informers".

Tradition has long since dictated the roles man and woman perform in society. Most cultures are heteronormative in nature – that means that man and women marry each other and then raise a family together, and when they *do* do so, their roles are clearly defined into the idea of the domestic and the non-domestic.

Of course, today, times are changing and the idea of the family unit itself is far more progressive than it was even as early as a few decades ago. Still though, even in today's modern world, the woman is perceived to be a delicate flower, genteel and beautiful and small – something to be protected and looked after.

Conservative societies even now would rather that the woman sticks to the domestic instead of working her way into the world and creating a space for herself, this stereotype has continually been reinforced by the media and other sources.

World War Two Women

What man tends to forget – is that women are brave and strong and can withstand far more than what we would think them capable of. A woman is capable of bringing *life* into the world; she is just as capable of *ending* it, or changing it in ways we would never imagine.

Clichéd though it may be, a human being's true strength of character is reflected in the most difficult of times. The world had to sit up and take note of just how strong a woman could be when the two world wars hit.

Even taking the side of the traditionalists, one could deny that women were as important to the war as men were. This so called weaker sex had to fight their own battles within their homes – their husbands, fathers and brothers went to face the enemy on the front lines while they fought tooth and nail to keep the family running.

The men's enemies had faces and could be eradicated; the women fought the nameless powers of hunger and poverty. They kept the families safe and running until the wars ended.

And still more women went to the actual battlefront itself! Women had a unique advantage over the men; they could blend into the background seamlessly, precisely because of the prevalent sexist attitudes of the times.

Nobody would accuse a sweet, innocent looking little girl of being a spy who was transmitting information back to her employers. These courageous ladies risked their lives daily – particularly in the Second World War – and saved millions of innocent people. They are often not given enough importance and are outshined by their male counterparts.

Their bravery, their self-sacrifice and their daring cannot be forgotten, for without them, the War could have been lost and the world we live in today could be a very different place.

This book chronicles the stories of four such women – Noor Inayat Khan, Krystyna Starbek, Virginia Hall and Pearl Witherington – all of whom put their lives on the line for their countries. They made no apologies or excuses about who they were and quietly went about changing the face of the war, helping the Allied Powers take on the power-crazed men of Nazi Germany and come out victorious.

Thank you for purchasing this book! I hope you find it

World War Two Women

informative!

Chapter 1: Pearl Witherington – The Leading Lady

Born Cecile Pearl Witherington on the 24th of June in the year 1914, she was one of the few women spies who survived the war and lived a long, fruitful life. She lived through the horrors of the violence and came out – not unscathed – alive to tell the tale.

Her own story is something to be admired; she was one of the most dangerous female spies to have ever lived, taking on the Germans fearlessly and risking her own life time and again to save as many innocents as she could.

Humble beginnings

Her tale begins in France, where she was born, despite that, she was a British subject and worked at the British embassy in Paris. Her life was a struggle even when she was young. He father was a heavy drinker, and he threw away most of his money, leaving them to a hand-to-mouth existence.

Witherington had to start working as early as 17 years old and she earned extra money by teaching English at the night school. Her life was not entirely unhappy, however;

she was engaged to be married to man called Henri Cornioley and they were quite content together. It was in May 1940 that her life changed – Germany invaded France.

The occupied country meant that the embassy she worked in shut down and she did not have a job any longer. As British subjects, the lives of Witherington and her family were in constant danger; they kept a low profile, but the German troops began to round up British nationals soon enough.

This meant that she had to flee; her mother and her sisters accompanied her as they left France. They went to an American consul for help and once their visas to Spain and Portugal were fixed, they left France for good. A long, frightening journey later, they were in London, where she took up work in the Air Ministry.

The fight against the Germans

At the Air Ministry, Pearl Witherington came into contact with an old friend of hers – Maurice Southgate. Both of them shared a stark hatred of the Germans, who had taken over their home and both wanted to do something to bring liberty back to their people.

Southgate forged on ahead, going on to join the Special Operations Executive – the SOE – in the year 1942. A quick note on the SOE – this was an organization that worked behind the scenes during the Second World War.

It recruited men and women to sneak beyond enemy lines and spy on them, while transmitting information back to the Allied Powers. They also worked with the locals in occupied countries to put up resistance to the Axis Powers.

Witherington wanted to follow him into the world of spies, but it was not easy for her. It took almost a year, but finally, in 1943, she too joined the Special Operations Executive and officially became an agent. Working with the SOE meant that she would have to train herself in all manners of things – from handling weapons to creating new cover identities.

Witherington did not shy away from it; she embraced it with fervor, going so far as to emerge *'the best shot'* the service had ever seen.

She was smart and intelligent; it did not take her long to identify what her trainers were looking for. Her French was excellent and added to that was the fact that she was direct, honest and calm in the face of difficulty. As someone who had grown up in a tumultuous family situation and had heralded her entire family into safer waters, she knew how to keep a cool head and look at things from a detached, unemotional point of view.

All those things gave her an unexpected edge, and she breezed through her training sessions with flying colors.

When her training was over with, it was time for her to embark on a mission in occupied France. She returned to her home – but not as herself. The code-name she was designated was *'Marie'* and she was dropped into occupied France by parachute on the 22nd of September 1943.

There were spy networks all over the country, running under code-names and working closely with one another to quietly dismantle the German troops and take on the Gestapo from behind scenes. She joined one such network – the STATIONER Network, headed by Maurice Southgate. Like most beginner spies, she worked as Southgate's courier.

Pearl Witherington's return to France marked her

reunion with not only her childhood friend, but her long lost fiancé as well. The Germans had captured Henri soon after she had fled the country; he had escaped their camps and then joined Southgate's network.

In the following months, they worked together as spies for the Allied Forces, and he became her right hand later when she headed her own network.

Her work with the network was not easy; she started working as Southgate's courier first. On her first tour of his groups, she was worried that the Maquis men would have problems learning arms training from a woman.

Fortunately for her, they were desperate and really had no choice but to accept help. It wasn't long before she earned their respect, however, considering how good a shot she was and how good a solider she could be.

Her work in dealing with the Germans and their organizations led to the formation of a whole new spy network called Freelance. But the job was not easy; she was beginning to feel the strain of being constantly vigilant and maintaining a cover, along with long journeys and regular Gestapo checks. There were times she had no place to stay and she had to resort to sleeping in train carriages that were extremely cold.

D-Day, though, was fast approaching, and with it, the end of the war itself. In January of 1944, Maurice Southgate had new orders – he had to help in the building of a secret army to keep the Germans at bay when D-Day did arrive. Unfortunately for him, he was able to do little – their network, STATIONER, collapsed.

Southgate, wearied from too much work, walked right into a Gestapo trap. He was then sent to the Buchenwald concentration camp, where he remained for almost a year before the American forces liberated the prisoners there.

Pearl Witherington spread news of his arrest as quickly as she could, knowing his entire network would be in danger. The network was then disbanded, and Witherington moved to a new network, WRESTLER.

She did not just work there – her experience meant that she became the leader of it, under the new codename, 'Pauline'. Having been reunited with her fiancé, Henri Cornioley, she took his help to reorganize it, setting it up the way she liked to help as many as she could.

She was the only woman to become a network leader,

though there were women like Andree Borrel who were second in commands to their male counterparts.

She included members of the Maquis, who were rural guerilla warriors who had escaped into the mountains to avoid the Germans. They were locals, and adding more than one thousand of them to her network meant that Witherington had access to a lot of information and supplies and a direct way to hit the enemy.

The Maquis were instrumental in the D-Day attack on the Axis Powers, and Witherington had recognized their importance earlier on. She knit them all close together, and put them to work.

Resistance in the rural area of France was weak, though. They were unorganized and many of them did not want anything to do with Londoners. It took all of Pearl Witherington's wit to bring them together and train them to take on German forces.

Her ideas were so successful and the plan so efficient that the Germans sat up and began to take notice. They tried to suppress the Maquis, but to no avail. Witherington lead them with grit and determination they had not expected and in the end, they were so frustrated with her, they put up a 1,000,000 franc bounty on her head.

They wanted her gone and did everything they could to stop her, including ordering an attack on her.

2000 German soldiers descended on Witherington and her force. The Maquis, though fierce fighters, were not strong enough to take on such a large, trained force and had to give in. The battle lasted close to 14 hours, but Witherington had to flee and hide until the Nazis left.

The invaders burned down farms and houses, but they did not know how to retaliate against the guerilla warfare of the locals, who held them off. Unfortunately, the next day, they returned to burn down the Wrestler network's arms dumps.

Pearl Witherington was left with nothing, and had to regroup and start from scratch. She was not giving up, though, she sent a request back to London for military support, but they were unable to help, which meant that she would have to set it all up for herself.

It was not easy; she called and arranged for supply drops and orchestrated no less than 13 parachute operations. Through this, she had collected enough weaponry to arm the force of the 1500 men she had built up. She continued to train them until the end of July, when at last, a French commander showed up to help her organize the Maquis attacks on German convoys.

What intelligence they had on the local train movements was good; it allowed them to consistently disrupt the trains and destroy petrol wagons bound for Normandy.

The Germans continued to try and hunt Witherington down but she gave back as good as she got. A large scale guerilla assault was set up on the Germans who were traveling through her area of operation. The small force she led into battle killed close to a thousand German soldiers.

They disrupted a key railway line that connected the south of France to Normandy more than 800 times – they were relentless, particularly in the month of the D-Day, as though they sensed the end of the war approaching rapidly. They attacked German convoys regularly and posed a real threat to the Nazis, despite being a very small force in comparison to the Germans.

Finally, in mid-September, much after D-Day, Pearl Witherington's Wrestler network bore witness to the surrender of the remaining 18,000 German troops. That they gave themselves up was a testament to the strength of her leadership; she had led them to victory against all odds.

What was even more surprising was the integrity and the honesty with which she handled her duties. When Witherington returned to London, she not only turned in her missions reports – as was required of an agent – but also submitted a report that offered a breakdown of all her expenditures on the field.

It listed in detail every purchase she had made to support her war effort, from cigarettes to razor blades. The report was one of a kind and much appreciated, leaving all her critics stunned and speechless.

Pearl Witherington did not stop fighting even when the war was over. During the battle, she had taken on Nazis and Germans and real life soldiers against whom she could wield weapons.

Once it was over though, she had to fight to be respected as a woman – as evidenced by her response to the *Order of the British Empire* she was offered but turned down. Initially, her name was recommended for nothing less than the *Military Cross* itself – a high honor given to men who performed exemplary gallantry acts on the battlefield.

She was rejected for this, since she was a woman and it was then given only to males. Instead, she was offered the *MBE (Civil Division)* and she flat out refused it, pointing out rather coldly that there was nothing remotely *'civil'* about any of the things she had done. In the end, she would take nothing less than a military MBE.

The life after

The French awarded her the *Croix de Guerre* and the *Legion d'honneur*. To Witherington, however, the most important honor she would ever receive was the parachute wings. She had completed three training parachute jumps and one more operational jump.

To receive them, however, the candidates had to do four training and one operational jumps – she had been a single jump short of receiving what she had dreamed of. She bemoaned her fate for close to six decades before her wish was finally fulfilled and she was awarded with her wings.

Pear Witherington returned to Paris where she started her lifelong career at the World Bank. The war was over and she no longer needed to be a soldier. So she went home and married her fiancé, Henri Cornioley in October of the year 1944.

They had fought and survived a war together, and their relationship was cemented by the trials and tribulations they had weathered. She gave birth to a little girl soon after, whom they named Claire.

In fact, that she and her lover lived through a war and stayed together has made many a spectator swoon at the romance of it all. Some even say that their love story – not quite the regular Mills and Boon fairytale – served as the inspiration of Sebastian Faulk's popular novel, *'Charlotte Gray'*.

Pearl Witherington Cornioley herself refused to see it as such. She declared that it was not romance that pushed her to fight a war; in an interview with *The Telegraph* in the year 2002, she said, *"There was a job to be done. I didn't put my life at risk just so I could be with Henri."*

Still, their relationship is one to be admired – they stayed together till his death in the year 1999. The soldier turned pharmacist was no doubt the love of Pearl Witherington's life, who lived past him into the twenty first century. Their legacy, though, was not just the war and the suffering – they established a memorial in Valencay in the year 1991, commemorating the 104 F Section agents who did not return home from their missions.

After Henri passed away, Witherington became the honorary president of the *Federation Nationale Libre Resistance*, which was an organization set up to remember and honor the F Section agents and staff.

Pearl Witherington lived a long, fruitful life, remaining a strongly opinionated woman, whose presence was magnetic. She was vocal about her disapproval of the romanticized portrayal of the women spies of the SOE in the Second World War, and did not often open about her own exploits in the war. She was a woman of integrity and honesty, who lived a simple life.

Her wartime experiences left her wise old soul, who survived to the age of 93. It was only in the February of the year 2008 that she breathed her last, having left an indelible mark on the world.

Her contribution to the war effort cannot be trivialized;

without her, winning the war against the Nazis would have been extremely difficult, if not altogether impossible. She was strong, brave and an excellent leader – she was a woman, and proud of it, refusing to bow down to anybody and instead using her intelligence and strength to stand up for what she believed in.

Chapter 2: Virginia Hall – The Limping Lady

Fighting a war with all your facilities is hard enough; war is hard, demanding of the person of both physical and mental requirements beyond what they can give.

Virginia Hall, on the other hand, was a soldier who fought the Nazis – with a single foot. She was a woman with a single foot and a mission; she did not care that she was physically handicapped, only that she continue to fight for what she believed in.

Background

Born on the 6th of April in the year 1906, Virginia Hall was an American spy, who worked with the Special Operations Executive – like most female spies. But her career as a spy did not end there; she would go on to work with the American Offices of Strategic Services and then the CIA (Central Intelligence Agency) itself. The Germans thought her to be the most dangerous spy of all time – with good reason.

Virginia Hall's story begins in Baltimore, Maryland, where she took her first breath. She went to Roland Park

Country School and attended Barnard College, where she learnt French, Italian and German.

That she knew so many languages would come in handy later – right then, she wanted to see Europe and finish her education there. She took to traveling and spent time in France, Germany and Austria, studying and learning, as she wanted to, before finally becoming a Consular Service clerk at the American Embassy in Warsaw in Poland.

The accident

Hall's initial plan had been to join the Foreign Service, but she sabotaged her own dream when she accidentally shot herself in the leg in the year 1932. The injury left her crippled; her leg had to be amputated from the knee down, leaving her with a cheap prosthetic.

She took it in good stead, though, trying to adapt to being one-legged as best as she could, even going so far as to name her prosthetic, *'Cuthbert'*. With an injury like hers, her diplomatic career was all but over.

She resigned from the Department of State in the year 1939, and took up studying again, going to graduate school in the American University in Washington DC.

When the Second World War came around, she was in Paris. Watching so many suffering around her, she could not resist joining the Ambulance Service, and this was just before France fell to German forces. She became an ambulance driver to pull the wounded away from the battle.

It was no small feat, considering that she had only one leg and had to maneuver the ambulance in ways that was no doubt painful to her hurt leg.

The spying

The experience definitely did not put her off from the war; if anything, it made her even more determined to extend a hand to those fighting in the front. She went to London – the Special Operations Executive had just been formed and she jumped straight into the forefront with them.

The SOE sent her back to France, to Vichy, where she spent about 14 months, helping to coordinate the activities of the French Underground networks. Her cover was that of a correspondent of the *New York Post*.

She helped many downed fliers of the Allied Powers

escape, performed the services of the couriers for the spy networks, obtained supplies and forged identities for other spies. She also had to maintain her own cover, which meant that she was filing regular articles to *the Post*.

Her actions were bound to get her noticed; the Germans knew of her, and put up posters for her capture. In the year 1942, when Germany completely occupied France and took over the country, Hall had to flee to Spain. By then, she had garnered quite the reputation – the Germans would give anything for the capture of the female spy they dubbed *'The Limping Lady'*.

She had made it into their Most Wanted list, she had to walk across the snow-covered Pyrenees to reach Spain, and spent the next year working in Madrid for the Special Operations Executive since it was definitely too dangerous for her to go back to France.

The beginning of Diane

After her return home, she joined the United States Office of Strategic Services (OSS) Special Operations Branch in the year 1944. She wanted to get back to a still-occupied France, and requested her superiors to do so immediately.

Considering her skills and the amount of clandestine experience she had, the OSS did not hesitate to fulfill her wishes.

They provided her with a forged French identification, giving her the codename *'Diane'*, and landed her from a British MTB in Brittany. Her injured leg meant that she could not parachute in, but that did not stop her from jumping metaphorically right back into action, contacting the French Resistance in central France while avoiding the Gestapo.

This time too, her help in the war was as invaluable as it had been previously. She mapped out drop zones for supplies and built and coordinated safe houses for the refugees and the wounded.

In the guise of an elderly farmhand, she organized sabotage operations and organized the resistance groups. She helped three battalions of the Resistance to fight a guerilla war against the Germans on their own and continued to gather intelligence and send it back to the Allied Forces, who could not have defeated the Axis Powers in her absence.

The happy ending

With her help, the war drew to a close with Germany's defeat and Virginia Hill returned home to America. In the year 1950, she married a fellow OSS Agent, Paul Goillot and the following year, she shifted to the CIA, where she worked as an intelligence analyst, particularly on the French parliamentary affairs.

She and her husband worked side by side later in the Special Activities Division of the CIA – her career in the intelligence community was long and fruitful. She only retired in the year 1966, moving to a farm in the Barnesville, Maryland.

Virginia Hill was honored with a number of awards for her bravery and work in the war. The most important of these was the *Distinguished Service Cross*, which was given to her by none other than General William Joseph Donovan himself.

She lived a long and fruitful life, passing away at the ripe age of 76 on the 8th of July in the year 1982. Virginia Hill may have been a physically handicapped person, but she was more of a whole and full person than most normal people. She stood up for what she believed in and refused to give into the demands of her mangled body, instead forging on ahead.

Never once did she let her injury stop her and without her assistance, the war would have been almost impossible to win. The Limping Lady certainly left her footprint in the sands of time!

Chapter 3: Krystyna Skarbek – The Woman With Many Faces

Born Maria Krystyna Janina Skarbek, this Polish woman was one of the most decorated women spies of the Second World War, who became famous for her daring exploits and her out of the box thinking when it came to her missions.

She took her first breath on the 1st of May in the year 1908, in Warsaw. Her father was a Count named Jerzy Skarbek and her mother, Stefania was from a wealthy family. Not only was she from an affluent background, she was also related to some famous personalities, including Fryderyk Skarbek, the prison reformer.

The Background

Krystyna's elder brother, Andrej, took after his mother and her side, but Skarbek herself was close to her father. She shared his love of riding horses, and even from a young age, she was breaking the delicate woman stereotype, choosing to sit astride rather than side-saddle as was expected of females who did ride.

Her athleticism was not restricted to riding alone; she was

an excellent skier – a skill she developed and perfected on visits to Zakopane in the Tatra Mountains. Her father encouraged her exploits so they shared a close rapport.

With the Great Depression, the family hit hard times and their finances were in trouble. They were forced to give up their estate and soon afterward, in the year 1930, Krystyna's father passed away. She was only 22.

There was very little money and to support her widowed mother, Krystyna took up a job at a Fiat car dealership, trying to earn what she could. Unfortunately for her, she fell ill from the automobile fumes and could not last long at the job. The prognosis doctors gave her was tuberculosis; her father had died of the disease as well.

Luckily, her employer had to compensate her with her medical insurance, and with the money, she supported her family.

To make sure she remained healthy, her doctor advised her to spend as much time in the open air as possible, and Skarbek took to spending most of her time in the Tatra Mountains, hiking and skiing. It was where she had grown up, where she had learned to ski and spent time with her father – she felt at home there and the peace helped her remain healthy.

The affairs

She had a couple of beaus the same year, though nothing amounted to fairy tale romances. She married Gustaw Gettlich, a businessman, but they had a mutual divorce; another love affair also failed when her prospective husband's mother refused to accept a poor, divorced woman as her daughter in law.

One of the few times she actually lost control of her skis on the slopes, she was saved by a giant man named Jerzy Gizycki, who stepped right into her path to stop her from crashing.

He was an irascible eccentric, who had run away from his wealthy family in Ukraine and gone to the United States where he had worked to make a living. Eventually, he had become a writer and traveled the world doing research for his books.

In 1938, Krystyna married her strange, eccentric savior, following which he accepted a diplomatic posting to Ethiopia. There he maintained the position of Poland's consul general for almost a year until Germany invaded

Poland.

The First step

When the war began in earnest, Krystyna and her husband went to London, where she offered the Allies her services to fight the Germans. Initially, the British were not interested in her, but soon enough, they were convinced by her contacts to allow her to join them. Journalist Fredrick Augustus Voigt introduced her to the Secret Intelligence Service (SIS), and her career as a spy took off from there.

In 1939, she returned to Poland, which was now occupied by Germany. She convinced the Polish Olympic skater, Jan Marusarz, to escort her across the snow-covered Tatra Mountains, and take her to Warsaw, where her mother still remained.

Meeting up with the last parent she had, she begged her to leave the country with her, knowing her mother was in danger from the Nazis. Stefania Skarbek flat out refused to come; she wanted to stay where she was and continue teaching French to the little kids as she was doing currently.

Skarbek could not do anything about it; her mother would never see the freedom she herself had experienced, instead dying in a Warsaw Pawiak prison that the Germans had taken over. Ironically, it was a prison designed by none other than her own great-uncle, Frederyk Skarbek, who had been a prison reformer years ago.

On that first visit to Poland, Skarbek also was recognized by one of her old acquaintances – hazard for any spy in the field returning to their home country on a mission. The woman saw Skarbek in a café, and hailed her down, calling out to her loudly.

When Krystyna denied being who she was, the lady insisted it was her, but Krystyna managed to convince her otherwise. Thankfully, it did not result in disaster for the spy; she waited for a while in the café after the woman had left to avoid suspicion, and then got up to leave herself.

From Poland, Skarbek traveled to Hungary, where she encountered a childhood friend, Andrzej Kowerski, or – as he insisted on calling himself – Andrew Kennedy. He was a Polish army officer who had lost his leg in a hunting accident.

He worked as an extractor, bringing Polish and other Allied soldiers to safety, while gathering what intelligence he could. They spent some time together, but were arrested by the Gestapo in January 1941. In the moment when their lives were threatened, Krystyna showed a calm face in the face of disaster, negotiating their release.

She bit through her tongue until it bled and then showed it to the guards, pretending that she was presenting symptoms of pulmonary tuberculosis. The Germans, who had no wish to fall sick themselves, let her and her partner go and they escaped from Hungary via the Balkans and Turkey.

Skarbek then went on to organize a system of Polish couriers who collected intelligence and brought it from Warsaw to Budapest. She herself served as a courier, gathering intelligence when she could. Tales of her exploits during this time are quite popular; how true they are is something we can only speculate.

For instance, one story holds that she tricked a Gestapo officer into smuggling British propaganda for her into Poland. She told him that it was tea bought for her sick mother on the black market; the officer, charmed by her sweet smile and the story of the devoted daughter, went straight on to help her, taking the package into Poland himself, not realizing that he was helping the Allied Powers themselves.

Another story claims that on one of her trips to Poland, German soldiers detained her. To escape, she pulled out two live grenades that she threatened to detonate if they would not let her go.

To prove her point, she even removed the pins, being ready to kill herself as well the guards, if need be. The guards, obviously terrified, let her go immediately and she escaped.

The reality of these many stories is questionable, considering that most world war tales of heroism and sacrifice tend to be drawn out and exaggerated. Despite that, the truth is that Skarbek kept her wits about her no matter the danger she faced, and pulled herself and her companions out of sticky situations more times than one can count. She and Kowerski moved on from Poland, returning to their duties with the SOE.

When the two of them arrived at the SOE offices in Cairo in Egypt, however, suspicion fell on Kowerski, who was thought to be a German spy. Skarbek herself was also cast under suspicion and they had to face a number of inquiries to confirm their loyalties.

Skarbek had managed to easily acquire transit visas through Syria and Lebanon, which were French-mandated with the help of the Vichy French consul in Istanbul. It was believed that German spies could only get that done with such ease, and they accused her of being a spy.

Kowerski, on the other hand, had been cast as a spy since he had not reported to his superior. It took a while for the misunderstandings to be cleared up, but eventually, both Kowerski and Skarbek were cleared of all their charges and returned to their intelligence work.

The fall of another relationship

Skarbek's relationship with her husband, however, failed. When Gizycki was told of the charges leveled against her and Kowerski, he resigned his own career as a British intelligence agent in a show of support.

Unfortunately for him, though, Skarbek was not in tune with him; she told him that she had fallen in love with

Kowerski on their trip. Gizycki left her and went to London, eventually moving to Canada. They were divorced in Berlin on the 1st of August in the year 1946.

The French Connection

Before the official divorce, however, many more things were to happen in Skarbek's life. Her personal life was taking a hit, certainly, but her professional life as a spy was getting more exciting and dangerous as the days went by. Since she could speak excellent French, the SOE sent her to France, under the name *'Madame Pauline'*.

There were not enough trained operatives to send to the country to get it ready for the upcoming D-Day, and Skarbek's help was very welcome. New spies were in training but that was going to take a lot more time than expected. If they were sent into battle now, they would only end up comprising themselves as well as the SOE operatives already in place.

They needed to learn the skills they would require for survival first, and that was going to take more time than they could afford at the moment.

Skarbek, on the other hand, was already experienced, and

she had survived successful missions into the occupied countries of Europe. Moreover, she had shown brilliant skills in the face of imminent threats, being able to get herself and her companions out of sticky situations without the slightest hint of panic.

There was very little actual training she would have to undergo; only the smallest brush ups of her skills and she was good to go right back into battle!

Skarbek was chosen to replace fallen SOE agent, Cecily Lefort. Lefort was captured, severely tortured and eventually executed by the Gestapo. Skarbek would be a courier on a busy spy network that would be the first to meet the proposed Allied landings.

Unlike most of the women spies in France who answered to the F Section of the SOE, Skarbek's mission was launched from the Algiers, the base of AMF Section. Her lack of training with the SOE in itself was unusual; the AMF added to the mystery that was her spy career, separating her from the traditional female spies of the era.

For those who do not know what the AMF is – it was another section of the SOE set up in North Africa, with staff from the F Section in London and the MO 4 Section in Cairo working together there. It was set up because it was safer to run re-supply operations from Allied North Africa than the German-occupied France.

Skarbek worked with them and with their backing, took to her mission in France with fierce determination. She was to coordinate the resistance effort in southern France before the Allied Powers' invasion could begin. She was smart and did not hesitate to take risks, and it was no wonder that she rose quickly within ranks.

Her commanding officer was Francis Cammaerts, who was in charge of British liaison with the local resistance cells. Rumors were that the two were involved; Krystyna had many lovers, but none of them truly stuck, and whether this was true or not is left to speculation.

Cammaerts was captured along with two of his colleagues. At a checkpoint, one of the guards searched their things and found banknotes that had consecutive serial numbers. Now that would not be a problem generally, if not for the fact that they had claimed not to know one another.

They were arrested immediately; the guards did not know who they truly were or how integral they were to the resistance, but they had standing orders to take anybody suspected of being Allied Powers into custody.

When Skarbek heard the news, she turned to the local resistance men, and begged them to mount an attack on the prison to get them out. They refused, however, knowing it was a suicide mission, and Skarbek was left to her own devices. She was not going to give up, and came up with a brilliant – if reckless – plan.

Completely alone and without any backup whatsoever, she stormed into the captain's office and revealed her identity as a British agent. Captain Albert Schenck acted as a liaison of sorts between the local French prefecture and the Gestapo and she told him that she was the niece of the British General Bernard Montgomery, and ordered him to make sure that the prisoners were safe, threatening retribution if anything were to happen to them. She also offered him two million francs for their release.

She also bluffed that an Allied invasion was imminent, with the nearby town of Digne as the target – if he did not return the prisoners back to her. The only way the captain would escape death, she declared, was by liberating the prisoners and begging himself a pardon from the Allies.

Terrified, the captain arranged for her to meet with the Gestapo officer in charge – Max Waem.

What followed was a three-hour negotiation of epic proportions. Krystyna Skarbek was desperately trying to save her comrades while the Gestapo officer was doing everything he could to delay her and get her arrested as well. She dropped all pretenses, declaring that the full force of the Allies would be raining down on them at any given moment.

She herself was in wireless contact with the British forces, since she was a British parachutist and she would not return home without the prisoners. She pretended that Cammaerts was her husband, and she herself was British aristocracy, which meant that she held tremendous political influence.

Her threats seemed to work, especially when she invoked the name of the locals, who were not too fond of either man. The Gestapo officer – a lone man on his own without his army to protect him, faced with a woman of such apparent power – finally gave in and released the prisoners.

Captain Schneck himself was ordered to leave Digne following the release and the subsequent bribe that Skarbek had given him, but he refused to do so and was murdered later by an unknown assailant.

She had saved their lives by risking her own. Reportedly, a couple of years after the incident, she told another fellow World War II veteran that she had not given any thought to the danger her own life was in at all.

It was only after she and her comrades had made it out that she realized how easily she could have been killed. In her own words, she felt, *"What have I done! They could have shot me as well!"*

That she had performed so admirably and under such duress restored her reputation and put to rest any and all protests her critics had. When the SOE teams returned from France, a number of the British women were sent to fight new missions in the Pacific War, where the Japanese were still fighting the Allied Powers.

Skarbek, on the other hand, remained in Poland, serving as a courier for the final stage missions of the SOE within Europe itself. The Red Army – the Russian Army fighting for the Allied Powers – marched across Poland.

The Polish government, detained now that it was occupied by Germany, worked from underground with the British to create a new network of spies that would gather intelligence within the country.

Skarbek and her friend Kowerski – who had also regained his reputation and was welcomed back into the fold with open arms – were found to be integral to this mission. They were going to be dropped into Poland in early 1945, but the mission was called off, since the Red Army captured the first party that entered Poland, though they were released soon enough.

The end of en era

Soon afterward, the war drew to a close and Skarbek's military service and career as a spy also ended. Her exploits in the war had saved many lives; it was time to award her bravery and her wit in keeping herself and her comrades alive.

Her work in Digne won her the George Medal. The French honored her with the *Croix de Guerre,* and for the work she did with the British, she received the prestigious *Officer of the Order of the British Empire post (OBE),* which was a step above the *Order of the British Empire (MBE)* which was what most of the female SOE agents received.

Despite all the awards she claimed and the not-insignificant reputation she had garnered for herself, Skarbek's situation when the war ended was nothing short of pitiful. She did not have money to live on and she did not have a home to return to.

She had given up her country to join the Allied forces, never once making a home for herself away from the battle front. Sadly enough, she was given a single month's salary and then dropped in Cairo where she had to fend for herself. She applied for a British passport in the hopes of being able to return to England and make a living there, but bureaucratic administration delayed her, so she took to traveling instead, weaving her way in and out of difficult situations.

Skarbek was calm and cool during war and in the face of danger; peace confused her, especially without a home to help her find herself.

She made her way across the continent, in the end, returning to London after all. But she would go no farther than that; at the Shelbourne Hotel, Earls Court, an assassin stabbed her to death. She had just begun working as a liner stewardess with the Union Castle Line and had returned to London to relax after working a voyage out of Durban, South Africa.

The saddest part of the story is that her death had nothing to do with the war she had taken part in. It was not the death of the hero she had been, who had jumped into the battlefront with guns blazing and determination glinting in her eyes. It was a cheap death, given to her by an obsessed stalker, who thought he had any right to possess her.

Dennis Muldowney was a Reform Club reporter, who had proposed to her on the cruise. She had rejected him and unbeknownst to her, he followed her to London, where, angry that she had dared to reject him, he stabbed her to death mercilessly.

He was tried and convicted of her murder and then hanged to death himself on the gallows at HMP Pentonville on the 30th of September, 1952. Skarbek's body was buried at the St. Mary's Roman Catholic Cemetery in northwest London, and years later, when her brother died from cancer, his ashes were flown to her final resting place and scattered at the foot of her grave.

Krystyna Skarbek was a woman to be admired; she was calm and cool in the face of danger and never once stopped doing what she believed was right. She rarely took the time to look out for herself, focusing instead on how to keep her friends alive and then forging on ahead to defeat the enemy.

Rumors are that Ian Fleming was inspired by Krystyna Skarbek, and in his first James Bond novel, Casino Royale, had Vesper Lynd modeled after her. However, critics say that if this was supposed to be a portrayal of her, then it was a rather inaccurate one, considering that it was more a romanticized version of her story than anything else.

In the end, whatever she was, Krystyna Skarbek was a true warrior woman. She had a knife always strapped to her thigh, remaining ready for action at any given time, unafraid and unattached. She was strong and courageous; war did not leave her debilitated with fear as it did many others.

If anything, she was ten times smarter than many of her male comrades, jumping into action. She was not perfect;

she was reckless and a little bit of a daredevil, but more often than not, these qualities worked in her favor, getting her out of sticky situations where other people would have frozen up and lost their lives as a result.

Krystyna Skarbek – or Christine Granville as she preferred to be called – was an iconic woman, a warrior in the full sense. Being of the female sex did not deter her; she used it to her strength, flashing a thousand watt smile at many a German guard to get away safe and sound.

She was powerful and glorious and her actions saved many innocent lives. Her life, though, was lost to the whims and wishes of a possibly schizophrenic, madman who thought to possess her – and it is that madness in humanity that we need to mourn, as much as we lament the loss of such a wonderful woman herself.

Chapter 4: Noor Inayat Khan – The Warrior Princess

Most of the female spies who played an integral role in bringing the Nazi regime down in the Second World War were normal, middle class women, with families they had to provide for and still take on the enemy.

Noor Inayat Khan was an exception; her fight was of a different spectrum, given that she was no less than a princess and had responsibilities that went beyond just her family alone.

The royal story

Born Noor-un-Nisa Inayat Khan, this princess was a descendant of none other than the famous Tipu Sultan, the 18th century conqueror of the Kingdom of Mysore in Southern India. Her father, Inayat Khan was the eldest of four and came from a noble Indian family; his mother had been descended from the famous Indian King.

Despite the fact that they were royals, he did not spend much time in India, traveling Europe instead, teaching music and Sufism – a branch of Islam. Noor's mother was an American named Ameena Begum, who hailed from

Albuquerque, who met her father on one of his travels. They fell in love and got married and had Noor and her siblings.

Just before the First World War broke out, Noor and her family moved to London, where they lived in Bloomsbury. In the year 1920, they shifted again, this time to France, where they settled in Suersnes near Paris.

Her father passed away seven years later and the young girl took on the responsibility of caring for her grieving mother as well as her siblings, looking after them while pursuing her own degrees in child psychology and music.

To help out financially, she took to writing poetry as well as stories for little children that she sent out to magazines and radios, where they were published. In fact, she even had a book published – *Twenty Jataka Tales,* which was inspired by the *Jataka Tales* of the Buddhist tradition. The book was published in the year 1939 in London.

With the 1930s came the Second World War, and France was overrun by Germany. When the Nazis took over their home, Noor and her family had to flee from Paris to Bordeaux, where they traveled by sea to England.

Noor's father had been a pacifist; he had taught his children to aim for peace and turn their backs to violence. She was deeply influenced by his teachings and his beliefs; however, she and her brother, Vilayat, knew that if there were to be peace of any kind, the Nazis would have to be defeated.

Added to that was the fact that she herself was of an Indian descent; she stood against the British occupation of India at the time, which was fighting for its independence on the other side of the world.

Destiny's die had been cast – she *did* join the Allied Forces, but it could have easily gone the other way. Had her family remained in India, it is very possible that she would have been part of Indian Independence struggle instead of the Second World War.

In her own words, she said that she wished that, *"...some Indians would win high military distinction in this war. If one or two could do something in the Allied service which was very brave and which everybody admired it would help to make a bridge between the English people and the Indians."*

World War Two Women
The Participation in the WW2

To bring about the peace she hoped for, she joined the Women's Auxiliary Air Force – the WAAF – where she became an Aircraftwoman of 2nd Class. After that, she was sent for training as a wireless operator and later went on to join the Special Operations Executive, in the F Section. She underwent strict training in her post with the SOE, where she adopted the name *'Nora Baker'*.

A number of her superiors were ambivalent about her presence, but her French was fluent and her wireless operation was quite good, and so, they made her one of the many spies who operated in a German occupied France.

In the year 1943, with the code-name *'Madeleine'*, under the cover identity of Jeanne-Marie Regnier, Noor Inayat Khan was sent to Northern France, where she joined the PHYSICIAN Network headed by Francis Suttill. The network is also famous by the name of PROSPER, and two other women joined her – Diana Rowden and Cecily Lefort, both of whom would lose their lives in the war, just like Inayat Khan herself.

Unfortunately for her, troubles began as soon as she was

dropped behind enemy lines.

The PHYSCIAN network's radio operators were arrested by the Sicherheitsdienst (SD) along with a number of resistance fighters who were thought to be linked with prosper. Reports state that Inayat Khan refused to return to Britain, despite the danger; she was one of the few remaining wireless operator still outside prison, and that made the information she transmitted back to the Allies absolutely invaluable.

She reorganized what was left of the network and tried to coordinate their work, so much so that she made it into the Gestapo's list of most wanted British agents. SD officers searched for her high and low, and circulated descriptions of her within their officers in the hopes of capturing her.

Inayat Khan kept moving constantly to maintain her wireless connection with London; there were wireless detection vans that followed her and she had to evade them regularly to transmit information back to the Allies. Her job had become the most dangerous in all of France, but she refused to give up, since it was also the most important job within the country.

The capture

But it could hardly last forever. The good work she did came to an abrupt end; she was betrayed to the Germans by someone from within the network – rumors are that it could have been either Henri Dericourt or Renee Garry.

The former (codenamed Gilbert) was an SOE officer who had been suspected of working as a double agent. The latter's story is more melodramatic; reports say that she allegedly accepted 100,000 francs in return for betraying Inayat Khan, whom she was jealous of, since the princess had apparently stolen the affections of another SOE agent Garry had wanted for herself.

Whatever be the case, Noor Inayat Khan was arrested and then taken to the SD Headquarters, where she was interrogated. Her fierce determination to not be taken into custody belied her gentle nature; she fought them off so fiercely that they labeled her one of their more dangerous prisoners and had her interrogated for close to a month.

She tried to escape their custody twice, and refused to give out any information, instead lying her way through her interrogations.

Inayat Khan made one mistake, however. She herself had not revealed any details of her missions to her captors, but the SD found her notebooks. Contrary to security protocol, she had written down all the messages she had transmitted back to the Allies.

The Germans made full use of these details, going so far as to pretend being her to feed the Allies false information. London also made errors during this time; they did not authenticate these messages, and sent three more agents to France, who were captured even as they landed into the occupied country. What was worse was that London did receive news of Inayat Khan's capture soon after, but they ignored it.

Sonia Olschanezky, who was a local SOE agent, sent a message back to London, telling them of Inayat Khan's arrest. She insisted that Baker Street ignore any communications from *'Madelaine'*, and if possible, send a team to rescue her. Her message was ignored as unreliable since the home base did not know who she was; she was a local resistance fighter, and had little influence on the Allies.

This meant that the German transmissions were taken to

be Inayat Khan's actual communication, and it lead to the deaths of a number of SOE agents, including Olschanezky herself.

SOE agent Vera Atkins was sent to investigate the missing agents (who had been captured or killed by the Germans already) and initially, she mistook Olschanezky for Inayat Khan. The former had already been executed, but the latter was still alive, which she would come to realize only later.

The torture and death

In the meantime, Inayat Khan herself managed to escape the SD Headquarters where she was being held, along with two other SOE agents. However, they were captured before they could go far and Inayat Khan was taken to Germany for '*safe custody*'.

Her fate was sealed – she was cast under the '*Nacht and Nebel*' directive. This was the '*Night and Fog*' directive, under which she was condemned to disappear without a trace. It was a route left for the most dangerous of prisoners, and nobody who went in came out.

For ten months, Inayat Khan was kept shackled in

complete secrecy – nobody knew where she had been taken, or even if she was alive.

It was after the war that her prison director testified to her sad state of affairs; she was regularly tortured for information, but she refused to give in, not disclosing anything to the Germans. Other prisoners, he said, could hear her crying at night, but she remained strong in the face of her captors, keeping her lips sealed. Her happy ending was not meant to be, though.

On the 13th of September, in the year 1944, Noor Inayat Khan was executed, along with three other SOE Agents – Yolande Beekman, Eliane Plewman, and Madeleine Damerment.

They were all killed by a shot to the back of their heads; an anonymous Dutch prisoner claimed that he had watched Inayat Khan be beaten brutally by one of the guards, and it was very possible that her death was caused by the beating and not the gunshot itself. The bodies of the four women were then immediately burned in the crematorium.

Speculation is also rampant that Inayat Khan may have been tortured sexually for the information the Germans wanted, but there is little evidence to confirm or deny these accusations, considering there is no body to examine. Inayat Khan's last word is recorded to have been '*Liberté*'. It indicates clearly the strength of her character; she died for what she believed in and refused to give into torture.

Her bravery could obviously not go unmentioned. She had performed the most dangerous job in all of France and then held out for almost a year under pressure without betraying her loyalties.

For her self-sacrifice and bravery, she was posthumously honored with the *George Cross*; the French also bestowed the *Croix de Guerre* upon her, with a silver star. There is even a bronze bust of her, placed in the Gordon Square Gardens in London.

Noor Inayat Khan inspired a number of literary and art works. Her biography is being made into a film, and American poets, Stacy Ericson and Irfanulla Shariff both wrote poems dedicated to her and about her that are available online.

Even a Television miniseries was made, chronicling the life of Inayat Khan, though there were a number of inconsistencies, such as the lack of usage of her name as Nora Baker or the speculation about who betrayed her to the Germans.

Noor Inayat Khan was the least suitable person to become a spy. She was a pacifist and reports state that she outright refused to lie – as evidenced by her frank admission of her dislike of Britain during her interview with them. She claimed that she would finish this war and then fight for Indian Independence, and in all her activities, she advocated freedom and liberty.

Physically too, she was nowhere near what the trainers would expect from someone who wanted to be a spy. She found it difficult to stand up in mock interrogations.

And yet, it was this conundrum of a woman who helped the Allies win the war. She lasted for months all by herself in enemy territory, refusing extractions. She evaded German troops and outran the Nazis, doing the work of six people and relaying invaluable information back to the Allies without which the war would have been lost.

And when she was captured, the girl who could not lose more than an hour in mock interrogations, was kept prisoner for ten months, undergoing torture and possibly sexual assault.

Nor Inayat Khan was a *warrior princess* – she defied every stereotype of the fairytale princess and waited for no prince to rescue her. She served the people and stood up for her beliefs, wanting nothing more than to bring peace and happiness to the people around her.

Perhaps she never had the chance to rule a kingdom, but one cannot deny that she was a leader in the true sense – always looking for a way to bring peace to her home and to make sure everybody breathed the air of liberty and security. Noor Inayat Khan was a warrior princess to be remembered.

Conclusion

Thank you again for purchasing this book!

From the dawn of time, women have been accepted to be the creatures who kept the homes and took care of the babies. They are to be the nurturers to tend to the hearth and keep the domestic a place of sanctity.

But the truth is that women are capable of a whole lot more. They are as much fighters as they are caretakers; they are warriors as much as they are mothers and sisters. They are not as delicate as men would have them believe, capable of withstanding more pain than one could possibly fathom.

And it was these women who went out into the world and saved it. The Second World War could not have been won without the many female spies who were dropped into occupied territories, where they risked their lives time and again to relay information to the Allies, to gather intelligence or to save the fallen soldiers. The men fought the war with the women by their side and at their backs.

They also went in, guns blazing, when they needed to, never shying away from doing what needed to be done.

World War Two Women

They quietly maneuvered the war so that the Allied Forces could crush the oppressive regime of the Nazis, and in doing so, they changed the face of the world forever.

Who was going to suspect an innocent girl with a sweet smile, so delicate and soft? The spies took full advantage and as warriors and soldiers, they led their men to victory.

The women of the Second World War were fighters and protectors who carved for us the world we live in. We can never forget them!

If you enjoyed this book, do you think you could leave me a review on Amazon? Just search for this title and my name on Amazon to find it. Thank you so much, it is very much appreciated!

Other Books Written By Me

Below you'll find some of my other popular books that are popular on Amazon and Kindle as well. You can visit my author page on Amazon to see other work done by me. (Cyrus J. Zachary).

World War 2 Women

World War 2 Women – Book 2

World War 2 Submarines

World War 2 Submarines – Book 2

Holocaust Survivor Accounts

Holocaust Survivor Accounts – Book 2

Holocaust Rescuers

Holocaust Rescuers – Book 2

You can simply search for these titles on the Amazon website with my name to find them.

LIBRARY BUGS BOOKS

Like FREE books?

Would you like them delivered to you every week?

Do you like non-fiction books on a huge range of different topics?

We send out FREE e-books every week so we can share our books with the world!

We have FREE books every week on AMAZON that we send to our email list. If you want in, then visit the link below to sign up and sit back and wait for new books to be sent straight to your inbox!

It couldn't be simpler!

Www.LibraryBugs.com

If you want FREE books delivered straight to your inbox, then visit the link above and soon you'll be receiving a

World War Two Women
great list of FREE e-books every week!

Enjoy :)

Printed in Great Britain
by Amazon